With compassion and honesty, Lisa Moore inspires and shows us how to create a healthy lifestyle, make meaningful connections, and find beauty, grace, and redemption in the messiness of life. She shows us how to find the happiness that is inside each of us. Her wisdom and encouragement have challenged, clarified and deepened our understanding about what it means to be both parents and children.

– *Beverley and Gary Seehoff*

Lisa has the gift to put her finger on many sensitive topics that moving out from home entails. I find myself in so many situations highlighted in this book, thinking back to the time I left home to go off to college myself. Now, with the help of this book, I realize many patterns that were (and still are) part of my family's lives. If I had had this book back then, I – we – could have made some more "mindful" decisions, which could have saved us lots of arguments, tears, and drifting apart.

– *Helene Binder*

Reading Lisa's book has been an unexpected, emotional journey in every positive way. I read the book on a noisy flight with screaming babies and the hassle that comes with every transit, but it calmed me down immediately and made all the noise fade away. Once being a teenager who went through a huge transition to attend college in a different culture, I relate to so many challenges and thought processes that Lisa described in her interludes. Over the years, there were emotional struggles between my parents and I that I have already resolved, and Lisa's writing shed new light on them nevertheless. Being a business and life coach, I have also seen many such challenges reflected in my clients' struggles to discover themselves and embrace transitions. I can see the exercises of the book being applied in many different ways, to drastically diverse groups from different professions, cultures and at various stages of life transitions.

– *Chaoxiong You*

In her course, Lisa helped college students to overcome personal obstacles and fears. As I took her course, I was introduced to a variety of exercises to develop mindfulness and self-confidence. Lisa has extensive knowledge of different practices and provides thorough instructions on how and when to perform them. Activities ranging from drinking tea to performing the mountain pose helped me to put into perspective the bigger pictures in life. Lisa teaches her students to look past any previous struggles and to remain optimistic about the future. If not for Lisa Moore's course, I would still be struggling today. I personally credit her for helping me bring the calm into my life and for four smooth years in college.

– *Brian Kim*

THE
Mindful Guide
to College Preparation

A FIVE-DAY RETREAT FOR STUDENTS
AND THEIR PARENTS

LISA PALOMBO MOORE

With

S. R. Gilbert

Artwork by

Chaldea Emerson Deyman

BALBOA. PRESS

A DIVISION OF HAY HOUSE

Author Credits:
With S. R. Gilbert Art Work by Chaldea Emerson Deyman

Balboa Press books may be ordered through booksellers or by contacting:

Balboa Press
A Division of Hay House
1663 Liberty Drive
Bloomington, IN 47403
www.balboapress.com
1 (877) 407-4847

Because of the dynamic nature of the Internet, any web addresses or links contained in this book may have changed since publication and may no longer be valid. The views expressed in this work are solely those of the author and do not necessarily reflect the views of the publisher, and the publisher hereby disclaims any responsibility for them.

The author of this book does not dispense medical advice or prescribe the use of any technique as a form of treatment for physical, emotional, or medical problems without the advice of a physician, either directly or indirectly. The intent of the author is only to offer information of a general nature to help you in your quest for emotional and spiritual well-being. In the event you use any of the information in this book for yourself, which is your constitutional right, the author and the publisher assume no responsibility for your actions.

Any people depicted in stock imagery provided by Thinkstock are models, and such images are being used for illustrative purposes only. Certain stock imagery © Thinkstock.

ISBN: 978-1-5043-3376-4 (sc)
ISBN: 978-1-5043-3375-7 (e)

Library of Congress Control Number: 2015909566

Print information available on the last page.

Balboa Press rev. date: 08/04/2015

Contents

Bringing Mindfulness to the Entire Family

The summer after I finished high school, my father had a heart attack. He stayed in a Buffalo hospital for nearly two weeks. When at last he came home, he was thin and pale—and my mother did not look much better. After one glance at their faces, and one minute in that fear-filled house, I knew that neither had the strength to move forward. Their emotional tanks were empty, and so was mine. I realize only now, though, that we shared the same tank. Children and their parents usually do.

I come from a family of five. By the time of my father's illness, my brothers and sister had left home, allowing my parents and me to begin a new phase in our shared life together: friendship. Still, the final two years of high school had not been easy. I was questioning who I was and holding my self-image up to some pretty unrealistic ideals. Amid this turmoil, I could hardly wait to head off to George Washington University in Washington, DC. Like so many American teenagers, this would be my first time living away from home.

As August unfolded, my parents began cobbling together a routine. I was glad to see some type of rhythm return, but my own did not. For a long time, possibly all my life, it had been I, the child, who had carried my parents' emotions for them—their pain, their trauma, and their worries. And now, as I prepared to leave home, I took on the enormous fear that at any moment my father might die.

The summer inched along, and then, the week before the start of the fall semester, I made up my mind. I called the admissions office, explained what had happened, and said that under the circumstances I couldn't possibly leave my parents. I couldn't enroll that semester.

But wasn't I lying to myself? It is only now, thirty years later, that I realize the truth: I wanted to be appreciated by my parents. As an eighteen-year-old, I saw this great trauma as an opportunity to be seen and acknowledged as an individual. I wanted my father and mother to thank me for my help, for the sacrifice I made. That never came. Over the year that followed, this painful truth came into focus. I went away to college to see if I could exist without them because I did not exist with them.

Now that I am a parent myself, with children fast approaching college age, I have written a book for families who want to avoid a legacy of tangled and unspoken emotions. I want to open new pathways of communication—pathways that show a family how to be loving and supportive while granting autonomy to its individual members. For we don't need to take on one another's emotions in order to love, to be close, and to care. But in order to get there, we need to look carefully at our own experiences. I'll start with my own.

My parents had been wounded long before I knew them—childhood traumas, including some terrible tragedies in the world wars, had fragmented my father's family and left my mother's irreparably damaged. The only way my parents knew how to cope with emotional pain was to bury it. They bundled their parents' feelings up with many of their own and stuffed the whole mess into a sealed vault. This seemed to help, but it also generated a host of unhealthy reactive attitudes that had been passed along to me. *If I judge others, that'll ensure they will never get close enough to hurt me. If I remember the wrongs done to me, I will stay alert and safe. And if I bury all of this pain, I won't have to suffer.*

My parents and I are not alone. Once I was able to understand the emotional arrangement we had wordlessly orchestrated, I found it in many other families, including those of my students and my friends. Perhaps it's in yours. Children absorb the pain of their parents, as well as the coping strategies that go along with it. We fail to acknowledge deep and painful family wounds, and this prevents us from connecting with open hearts to our loved ones and to the world around us. Frequently, we embrace peers who are in similar distress. We look to bond through the darkness we know. And sometimes we cover our vulnerability with a haze of drugs and alcohol because that allows us to connect only in a guarded fashion that seems to keep us safe. But in following this path, we're less open to the world. We lose grip of our own truth, our own beauty, and our own joy.

Yet every part of this toxic process can be changed. The intergenerational cycle can be broken. But how? The secret is love—rediscovering the light and the love that are naturally within every one of us. Over five days, I'll introduce you to mindful practices that I've used in my own journey from buried emotions to greater clarity—to knowing who I was seeing in the mirror every morning. I'll lead you to a path on which parents and their grown-up children can deeply reconnect as they undergo an enormous change: the transition to college life.

For the past ten years, I've offered college students and those heading to college a time to reflect on their childhoods, their relationships with their families, and the changes they are going through as they enter adulthood. Every year, these students pour out their hearts to the groups I bring together, and they respond to the exercises I've devised with touching sincerity, vulnerability, courage, good humor, and, most importantly, curiosity about themselves. As I introduce students to my own version of the ancient practices of yoga, meditation, and general mindfulness, I see them change in front of my eyes, finding new paths to understanding and new courage to confront their fears. Just as importantly, I see them develop an inner calm and self-acceptance that are invaluable to them as they confront the enormous stresses that arise from their increasingly fast-paced, high-tech, interconnected, and competitive world. Students leave my workshops with the skills they need to understand who they are and how to uncover the happiness that lies within. I've kept in touch with many, many of these students. They universally report remarkable success by applying the methods of self-care that I've introduced to them.

As my teaching has progressed, I've realized that the type of mindfulness I emphasize can be just as meaningful for parents. So I've also developed workshops directed at parents going through the transition to college life—because as young people shed their high school skins to discover what lies beneath, parents also change. They become guardians and counselors to emerging adults, and they reevaluate their own life goals against a changing landscape. This moment offers a rare opportunity for the entire family to move together through an important life transition with greater focus, acceptance, and sensitivity, as well as with more mindful decision making. So this book is written for all of the "college bound"—for the young adults transitioning into a life at college and for those who are at home supporting these young adults as they make this exciting, but also anxious and bewildering, transformation. Holding this book, reading my words, commits the entire family to making this transition with mindfulness.

By "mindfulness," I mean the ability to pay attention in a sustained and open manner to the present—to the full depth of one's current experience, including the thoughts and emotions that are shaping it. But like anything of fundamental importance, mindfulness is difficult to grasp through a definition. So I'll show you what it is over the next five days.

In this short book, I'll introduce you and your family to five different practices drawn from ancient and modern tradition: tea drinking, mandala drawing, yoga, meditation, and journaling. Together, these practices provide an incomparable counterbalance to a fast-paced world, offering the solace and self-understanding so important to families in a time of change. We now have plenty of scientific research showing that in addition to a range of bodily benefits, these practices make beneficial changes to the brain, including improved ability to focus and significant reductions in stress. This will help the entire family as its members make difficult decisions, face big adjustments, and work to remain supportive during a time of change.

These practices are repeated with important variations on each day of the five-day retreat. As we move from one practice to another, we will travel between different states of mindfulness, growing accustomed to habits most workplaces and schools fail to cultivate, treating ourselves as the ultimate source of wisdom. For at its core, mindfulness involves trusting oneself, judging less, and coming to see that we're all connected. Once you trust yourself, you'll find that the answers to many of the most important questions are already right inside you. Eventually, you will need no system, no teacher, and no guru, because intuitively, you will know what is good for you: you are all you need. It's that easy.

Although I did eventually go to college, and my family did adjust, my own transition was difficult and incomplete. As I said, I'm completing it even today. If only I had known during that summer of transition what I know now … I wish I had been able to enter adulthood with mindfulness—with the practices and attitudes that I will introduce you to in this retreat. Yet, there is no loss in learning these lessons later. So be patient and loving toward your journey.

Finding a Time and Place

Set aside a time and a place for each day's exercises. You'll want a time of day when you feel rested, alert, and safe from interruptions. The first thing in the morning, before your day begins, generally works well, as can a quiet part of the evening. Try to keep to the same time each day; your body will begin to feel and welcome the rhythm. I developed the exercises so that they lead from one to the next. A calm and uninterrupted environment will deepen your experience. Hang up a "Do Not Disturb" sign for all to see. You should also give some thought to where you will do the exercises. The space should be quiet and as private as possible—a place where you want to be. Should you need a break, make it an invigorating walk, a wholesome snack, or maybe a warm bath.

I do not suggest a specific amount of time for all the activities. I feel this would take away from the deepest meaning of mindfulness. This time check is missing so you can pay greater attention to yourself and your internal life. If you start to worry about the time, just sit with that feeling and the emotions that it brings up. There is a wealth of information in every reaction you have during this retreat. Do the best you can to give yourself the greatest amount of freedom so you don't have to watch the clock.

Many of our days seem to be made of interruptions. Although we pride ourselves on our ability to multitask and switch course, this retreat requires something very different. You may not be able to take shelter in a shack built on the shore of a pond, but you can silence your telephone and turn off your computer. You might even consider unplugging each day for two hours before and after these activities. If you can make it through five days of being completely unplugged, go for it!

The Activities

TEA

Since I am not there with you, I want to offer something besides words. Here it is: the warmth of a **cup of tea**. As you brew the tea, pour it, inhale its earthy scent, and drink it, something close to meditation will happen, bridging your inner life and the outside world (not surprising, as tea has a deep connection with ancient practices). This opens the possibility of staying deeply connected to yourself while you move through your day. I offer specific tea suggestions for each day, but you should experiment with different varieties of tea, including old favorites as well as new flavors.

Several excellent mail-order companies now sell organic teas from China, India, Japan, and other countries.

Some like teabags; some prefer to buy loose tea and brew it in a pot. Either is fine. These teas are best without additions—except for chai, which will need either milk or a nondairy substitute, such as soymilk or almond milk. Find a mug that you like, that feels good in your hand, and that you can hold while your tea is hot, allowing the warmth to reach and embrace your palms.

MANDALAS

After you finish your tea, you can prepare your drawing materials. I provide a series of **mandala** outlines for you to color. Each has space for you to add your own artistic touches. A mandala is a sacred circle, a ring whose subdivided interior Hindus and Buddhists have long used to depict the universe. In addition to their remarkable spiritual resonance, mandalas possess healing powers supported by Western scientific research. Simply coloring a mandala can bring calm, which lowers your heartbeat and stills your thoughts. So put your crayons or colored pencils to work, making each drawing an expression of your playful inner child. Color outside the lines. Feel free to spill your tea and watch the paper absorb the lightly tinted liquid. You might even bring flowers in from the garden and use petals for color. Color these mandalas with pure joy.

MOVEMENT

Winding up your drawing, still in a relaxed and playful state from the mandala work, you will unroll a small mat and prepare to move through a series of basic **movements** called *asanas*. These yoga postures are not meant to tie you in knots, and I won't ask you to do headstands. Rather, these movements will help you focus on your balance and find the center of your energetic body. They are intended to slow you down so you can feel your breath entering your body. Use this as a time of inquiry, asking, "What part of my body does each breath touch, open, change?" As you grow aware of your own body, you develop an awareness that you can apply to your daily commute or walk.

I have studied many types of yoga over the past twenty-five years, and all are present in my descriptions. The poses I have chosen invite your mind to calm, affording you a greater awareness of your bodily sensations; this is a time to listen to the deep wisdom the body holds. It is an opportunity to put your mind aside and listen to your body. Free yourself of judgment, desire, ambition, and will. This is a time to surrender, not a time to ask questions or fix anything. Assume the poses in the way your body needs them. If you tend to push yourself, use these poses to listen to your body—to go only where it, and not your mind, wants to go.

For the movement exercises, a yoga mat is helpful, but any surface that is not slippery will work. The movement should be done in bare feet. I use the sounds of my breath and the environment to guide myself. Always listen for your inner voice. External music might conflict with your own internal voice and dilute the experience. Enjoy the peace and quiet.

Before you begin, take a minute or two to think about what makes up a yoga pose. The word *asana* simply means "sitting," and the early practitioners of yoga devoted themselves to maintaining a seated position for extended periods. As yoga evolved, a range of postures or poses was created. Yoga practitioners now move from one pose to the next, creating a linked series. Within each movement, there are *ulolas*, repetitive waves of motion. These simple and quiet actions create new neural pathways that allow a deeper connection with your body. These postures also make it easier to sit for longer periods of time while meditating.

If you ever feel uncomfortable, correct your pose by reconnecting your feet to the earth. Activate your entire foot—the ball, the length of each side of the foot, and the corners of the heels—and connect softly into the welcoming earth. This is more a matter of intention than of significant movement. Do the same with your hands. Allow the palms of your hands to be softly open and active, both when they are touching the ground and when they are not. This is the foundation of your practice, and reconnecting to your feet and hands will serve you well. If you still feel uncomfortable, adjust the pose to suit your body at that moment. You know best what you are capable of and how to protect yourself from injury. Listen to yourself.

As you move through the retreat, the yoga poses will build upon one another. When all five series of movements are combined, you will have created a routine known as moon salutation. My goal is to help you connect with your body, not push into a pose that will make you "strong," "sexy," or "desirable." This is about falling in love with yourself, not conforming to someone else's fantasy.

MEDITATION

After the series of movements, you will join me for a **guided meditation**. As I present it, meditation takes the form of play between you and your mind. A bit like the calm awareness that yoga can bring, these meditative reflections reveal how your consciousness works. They are meant to cast a spotlight on aspects of your everyday thoughts that you never really noticed. The meditations may not seem right for you initially, but if you simply read them every morning, after a few days or weeks, you will begin to notice dramatic changes in the way you perceive your world. Try setting a timer while doing these exercises. Five or ten minutes will do at first, but you'll find you want to increase the duration over time.

Try different sitting positions as you meditate. Find the one that is right for you. You will recognize it by a number of signals. The right position will make you feel safe and deeply connected to the earth, even if you're in a high-rise apartment. It will tell you that you're not running anywhere but staying put, with all your thoughts and feelings. Below are some suggested seating positions that you might try as you meditate.

Easy Posture

Kneeling Posture

Chair Posture

Easy Posture: Sit on a mat, carpet, or other comfortable surface with your legs crossed in front of you, close to your body, like you did in kindergarten. We used to call this "Indian style." Uncross your ankles if this feels more comfortable. Use a cushion under your bottom to raise your hips higher than your knees. This permits you to lengthen your spine, encouraging the natural curve in your lower back. Allow your shoulders to release away from your ears and your belly to soften. Keep your chin parallel to the ground, your palms on your thighs, and your eyes closed or downcast, looking about four feet in front of your legs.

Kneeling Posture: Kneel on a soft surface, and then sit back on your calves. You can try placing a firm cushion under your bottom, between your legs, to lessen the pressure on your calves. Feel your spine lengthen, the natural curve near your waist forming. Allow your belly to soften. Again, keep your chin parallel to the ground, your palms on your thighs, and your eyes nearly shut, looking about four feet out.

Chair Posture: Sit on a chair with a firm seat. You should be toward the front of the seat; your back should not rest on anything. Use a cushion if needed. Your feet should be firmly placed on the ground with your knees creating a right angle to your body—taller or shorter people will need to be judicious in choosing a chair. As in the other two positions, keep your chin parallel to the ground, your palms on your thighs, and your eyes closed or downcast, looking about four feet in front of your legs. Allow your belly to remain soft, your spine lengthened, fostering the lumbar curve in your lower back.

There is no reason to be uncomfortable while meditating. In fact, if you try different positions throughout the five days, it will become clear which posture is best for you. Remember things are always in motion. Listen to the wisdom of your body. It will guide you in finding a good meditation position, and changing it up when necessary.

JOURNAL EXERCISES

Each day ends with writing. These **journaling exercises** not only increase the connection between your mind and the inner you; they leave a record that you can consult in the future. While I've proposed topics that pull at the heartstrings of every individual on earth, in reality, you're doing no more than scratching the surface. As with the yoga and the meditation, I have offered a template for an ongoing practice. And as you build your own practice, finding new *asanas* and addressing new topics in your journal, you will find that they support you on your journey and invite you to enter into honest dialogue with your family.

Be sure to have sharp pencils or some pens available for the journal activities. You will write your reactions and thoughts directly into this book. I encourage you to keep a separate journal over the course of the retreat, recording all the things you did each day and, more importantly, what you felt and thought. Anything that comes to mind is worth setting down. Draw pictures and the designs that find their way into your conscious mind. This small journal will be a gift to yourself and a tool you can turn to in the future.

INTERLUDES

Interspersed among the descriptions of each day's suite of exercises, you'll find a number of **interludes** drawn from my own experience. In these, I explain through concrete experiences what I believe your family is going through. And I show how the methods I teach offer ways of listening to yourselves as your world changes. As you read my interludes, you might think about moments in your own life that felt similar and ask yourself whether a more mindful attitude might have allowed a different outcome.

Although the five daily exercises repeat, they develop over time. With each day, you step into a new role, assuming ever-greater responsibilities to yourself and your loved ones. Day 1 dwells on the emotional burdens often passed along from parents to children and how to become more aware of them. Day 2 addresses the difficult task of forgiving yourself and others. On day 3, we explore how to go about finding and understanding the wounds that we carry. On day 4, we begin to question what we believe and where these beliefs came from. The many insights we've gained from these first four days culminate in day 5, when we extend love and gratitude to ourselves and to others. Our five-day retreat is a foreshortened version of a much longer path you can pursue once you've mastered the practices presented in this book. Day 5 foreshadows a distant day, months, or years from now, when you will find the peace that so often eludes human beings.

A Checklist: What You'll Need for the Retreat

- tea: peppermint, rooibos, ginger, masala chai, and green tea
- art supplies: colored pencils (and sharpener), markers, pastel crayons, or watercolors
- yoga mat (if you are using one)
- notebook
- timer

1

The Trap

The school year ends, mortarboards get tossed in the air, and summer careens by. Before you've taken a breath, one of you is heading out the door toward a new life. But the whole family has been changed; as a teenager bursts into adulthood, every member of the family must forge a new relationship with each other and, crucially, with himself or herself. This transition is often overlooked because so many other things are happening. But it's also a wonderful opportunity to be mindful of our long-standing patterns of communication and our deepest emotions, not least anger and fear.

All around us lie a series of traps that can get in the way of understanding ourselves: busy work schedules, family obligations, extracurricular events, and even drugs, alcohol, and eating disorders. Today you'll step away from those to nourish a new beginning, where more mindful connections with one another allow strong emotions to show themselves in productive and healing ways. So let's get started!

Peppermint Tea

The first exercise of our first day begins with mint, a plant many find immensely soothing. I offer it to you as the gentlest of wake-ups, a promise of safety as you approach some new ideas and practices.

According to an ancient Greek myth, Minthe was the name of a water spirit who tried to seduce Hades, ruler of the underworld. To punish the spirit, Persephone, queen of the underworld, transformed Minthe into a small plant. But Persephone's vengeance was not absolute: few plants possess a scent as attractive as mint.

There are many ways to make peppermint tea. For today, you want something that contains no tealeaves, just mint. You can buy it in bags, but the best way is to pick some leaves from your own plant (about twenty is good), put them in a small pot, and fill the pot with boiling water. The tea—or tisane—is ready in moments. Perhaps your hands are a little cold. If so, fill a nice, big, ceramic cup with peppermint tea and take it in both hands, warming them.

Sit with your cup of tea and spend a few moments taking in the sharp, cleansing aroma. Notice your reaction to the scent. Maybe you love it, maybe you don't. Just notice your reaction. Does it make you feel calm or agitated? Just notice. Then, with mindful awareness, drink your cup of tea. Notice any sensations you have while you drink this tea. Are they pleasant, unpleasant, or neutral? Noticing is mindfulness. Mint awakens the senses. Use this time as an invitation to awaken yourself from within, to invite yourself, as an honored guest, to join your tea party.

Peppermint tea is naturally decaffeinated and has been shown to soothe an upset stomach, aid in digestion, relieve inflammation, and reduce nausea and diarrhea. Its clear and strong aroma prepares you for what we will do next.

Mandala Artwork

In Buddhist and Hindu art, the mandala is ubiquitous. Its encircling border, pierced by four portals, contains an inner sanctum with a lotus. Sometimes, it is painted; sometimes, it is made of colored sand. At other times, it is embroidered. Drawing and coloring mandalas is a widespread practice that heightens personal insight, healing, and self-expression. Interacting with these cosmic maps propels us along a path to the center of our being; what once was in shadow, the hidden and mysterious parts of our minds, is illuminated. If you're beset by internal struggles, you might take up your pencils and spend an hour with a mandala. You'll feel peace suffusing your mind, and the problems that worried you will become more tractable.

Mandalas function like maps offering views of the realm of enlightenment, gently suggesting pathways. For many, a mandala can be experienced like the paths of a labyrinth. The dead ends are the traps where we spend too much of our lives helplessly running into walls. Take the mandala as a symbol of your search, of a new awareness of the traps you want to understand and embrace.

As you choose colors to create your first mandala, try to express the way your heart feels right now. Ask yourself why you chose these colors. Is there a story to each stroke of the pen? You don't need to color within the lines. Add more shapes. Fill in the entire sheet. Joy!

Movement

CHILD'S POSE; EXTENDED CHILD'S POSE; ALL FOURS

Child's Pose

Extended Child's Pose

All Fours

INTRODUCTION

If at any time you feel uncomfortable, take a moment to adjust your body. Place your feet on the earth, picturing each foot extending into the four corners of a rectangle, even if your feet are not flat on the ground. Feel your entire foot—the ball, the length of each side of the foot, and the corners of the heels—connecting with the welcoming earth. This is more of an intention than a true movement. Relax and loosen your hands. Keep your belly soft. If you find that any of these movements do not support the needs of your body, alter them to suit you. You can use pillows for support or change the posture entirely. Keep it simple. Listen to yourself.

CHILD'S POSE

Begin this first yoga pose with your legs folded underneath you.
Your chest rests on your thighs.
Place your arms wherever they are comfortable.
Your forehead rests on the ground.

This is child's pose, the first part of the moon salutation. Breathe, noticing where your breath goes and what subtle movements it causes in your body. Where is your mind? Just notice, without judgment; just notice the state of your body and of your mind.

EXTENDED CHILD'S POSE

Extend your arms out on either side of your head.
Palms should be flat on the ground.
Elbows are softly raised off the ground.

Take a moment to feel your hands make contact with the ground. And feel, at the same time, the connection between the tops of your feet and the ground. Find a comfortable position for both your hands and your feet; they should feel alive and curious.

ALL FOURS

On an exhale, rise up onto your hands and knees.
Keep your back in a neutral, soft shape, your eyes lightly downcast.
Shoulders should relax away from your ears.

Take a few breaths here. Gently imagine your spine lengthening. This is visible only to your internal eye; it is an intention.

On an exhale, return to extended child's pose and bring your chest to your knees. Repeat these last two postures five times, from extended child's pose to all fours and back again. That's it.

This simple, repetitive movement is designed to calm your mind; you don't need to wonder what to do. This frees you to go into deep listening so you can better connect with your body and notice the activity in your mind. A complicated, challenging posture will not invite your mind to settle. The intention is to slow down and notice your internal life.

How did your body feel moving through these first poses? How did your mind react? I remember the first time I did a more meditative style of yoga. I was so agitated. I kept thinking, *How silly this is! Come on. I have been doing yoga for twenty years. This is such a joke!* I realize now that my reaction represented my need to run away from how I felt. This yoga invites your inner voice to start feeling like it might be heard. You may or may not like this. I didn't at first. But know that you are sowing the seeds to know yourself better and better.

Interlude

The Unhappy Outcome

A couple of years ago, I met a former student for tea. Lili lives far away, but a business trip took her to Boston so she put in some hours on the road to come visit. Over the four years we worked together while she was an undergraduate, we had become very good friends. It was a joy to reconnect.

Still, her news saddened me. Lili's father had fallen seriously ill, and she was planning to take a leave from work to spend some time with him. For some time, she had been putting emotional and physical distance between herself and her parents, along with the world she grew up in. She took a job involving lots of travel. She settled outside her native country. She adopted a new faith that was very different from her parents' set of beliefs, and she was engaged to marry a man of whom her parents did not approve. I can't think of anything else she could have done to show her parents that she had become her own person.

As we talked about these changes, I wanted to know what had fueled them. Lili seemed at a loss to offer an explanation, but she groped her way toward an emotion: resentment. Why had her parents refused to listen when she pleaded for their permission to study literature? Why had they insisted she major in economics when her heart wasn't in it? She was still angry about that, and that anger has shaped her life. Many of her decisions have been made in reaction to her parents—that is Lili's trap. Her own truth is unknown to her, buried under her reactivity and anger. Rather than acknowledge what is going on, she drugs herself with opera, theater, ballet, and museums, never giving a thought to visiting her aging parents.

I prodded a bit. Could her anger be traced to other resentments, other issues beyond her college major? As a child, for instance, had she been given permission to be herself? Had she been accepted for who she was? She looked at me with the saddest eyes, the eyes of a woman who had been denied a childhood, and she shook her head.

As parents, we might think our job is to mold our children. I know I've done my share of molding—always with the best of intentions. And children do need us to give them guidance, to serve as models of kindness and thoughtfulness. But always we must remain aware of their dreams, their impulses, their need to act as the compasses in their own lives. Sometimes, it's best simply to hold space for our children while we watch with wonder and joy as their lives unfold before our very eyes.

How to Meditate

Different traditions have fostered different types of meditation. I am going to convey to you the simplest and most universal type, an approach that has been shown in scores of studies to lower stress and resolve emotional disturbances. Mindfulness meditation (also known as Vipasannā meditation) opens us up to having a much clearer understanding of ourselves, enabling us to act with greater compassion and love. As you meditate, you open an understanding between your body and your mind, which invites an awareness that your body has a wisdom of its own. It has, in fact, all the answers you need.

Many things happen during our first days of meditation. A wandering mind, boredom, and sleepiness all come to call. Just notice these reactions. They are completely natural, and the most seasoned meditators deal with these very same distractions. Be curious about them. They don't indicate failure but progress. Noticing them is mindfulness.

So let's begin. Find a stable and comfortable position. I've suggested a few in the section on preparation. Squat, sit cross-legged on the floor, or sit on a chair. Your meditation position should tell your body and mind that you are not going anywhere right now. You are staying right here. You're safe.

Allow your shoulders to drop and your hands to rest easily. Your body must be comfortable. Meditation should never lead to struggle. If your legs feel awkward, please take the time you need to make them comfortable. Life brings us enough problems without creating more in meditation.

Allow your eyes to close or soften your gaze and look at the ground about four feet in front of you.

Now that you are comfortable, just sit, giving attention to your breath. You breathe all the time; nothing could be less eventful. Still, I am inviting you to be curious about your breath. Notice the pause at the beginning and the end of the exhale. Notice its tempo and rhythm. Notice its strength and its sound. If your mind wanders, as it does for all of us, just notice this too, and without judgment, bring your attention back to your breath. This is mindfulness—just noticing that your mind wandered. It's that simple.

Begin to feel your body. If you notice any areas of tightness, soften that area. Let your shoulders drop, relax your muscles to the extent you can at this time, and breathe freely. Be aware of your body as it rests in this meditation position.

As you sit quietly, you will notice different perceptions, as well as feelings and sounds that arise and pass. They are ripples in the ocean; they will subside. You are open and at peace.

As the meditation continues, return to your breathing. Feel its rhythm and the movement of your chest. Become aware of breath passing through your nostrils. If your mind wanders, just come back compassionately to your breath. As you now know, the moment that you notice your mind wandering, you experience mindfulness.

The life breath can calm us and restore us. Return to it again and again, meditating whenever you feel the need. When you're ready, open your eyes, and bring your attention back to the room.

Journal Activity: Minding the Trap

Mindfulness allows you to have a greater presence in your day-to-day activities. For example, when you are washing the dishes, you take notice of the water temperature and the feeling of the soap on your hands. Your mind is not planning or reliving the day's events. Notice what's going on in the present moment. Nothing more.

Now let's apply mindfulness to other events in our daily lives. For today's written exercise, think back over the last twenty-four hours. Allow some of the activities you've engaged in and interactions you've had to rise up in your memory. For this exercise, I want you to list three or four of the things that happened. They can range from "washed the morning dishes" and "brushed my teeth" to "won the lottery." You get the idea.

List those three or four activities below.

_____

_____

_____

Choose one of the activities from the list above and describe it with a bit of detail. Write your detailed description of this event below.

_____

_____

_____

If you could go back to that activity and redo it with greater mindfulness, would anything be different?

_____

_____

_____

Now think about a time spent with your family. Think of a moment when you saw a family member as somehow different from the rest of the group, essentially separate. Write a detailed description of this moment below.

_____

_____

_____

If you could go back to this moment and redo it with greater mindfulness, what would be different?

_____

_____

_____

Now think of a time when you or a family member was the subject of a joke, subtle putdown, or teasing. Write your experience below.

_____

_____

_____

If you could go back to that time and redo it with greater mindfulness and compassion, what would be different?

_____

_____

_____

When you or other family members diverge from family norms, are there love, support, and compassion for these individuals? Explain this below.

_____

_____

_____

How would greater mindfulness facilitate a change or bring greater support to family members that diverge from the family norm?

_____

_____

_____

Reflect on this exercise as you go to sleep tonight. Return to it when you wake up in the morning. See if you can bring greater mindfulness to the day tomorrow brings. Just try it.

Closure

The first day of the retreat is now over. We began by awakening our senses with mint, settled our minds with a mandala, assumed the posture of a child, and reflected on how mindfulness can be a part of our every day, helping us to avoid succumbing to the trap. The days that follow will be much like this, though we'll be discovering new areas of the heart and spirit that need special attention.

What separates today is the thought you have given to the trap, the way parents too often allow the pains and worries that burden them to affect their connections with their children. In fact, there are many traps, and my story about Lili, my former student, revolves around the trap of trying to impose your thinking on your children beyond their most impressionable years. For a college family, there is nothing more important than learning to see what's truly distinctive in each of us, valuing the traits that distinguish mother from son, father from daughter, and brother from sister. The goal is a series of discoveries about who we are.

I hope that many doors and ideas have shifted throughout this first day of your journey. If you feel unsettled, that's to be expected. Possibly, you felt nothing, which is also common. Much remains to be done.

Be gentle and kind with yourself. Place your hands on your heart and bow to your inner wisdom and strength. Offer yourself deep gratitude. I can't wait to show you day 2!

D A Y

2

Shame and Forgiveness

We all judge. We judge every day, in countless ways. The great Chinese philosopher Kongzi rhetorically asked, "Is there anyone who has managed to act with true goodness, using his entire heart, for even a single day?" He knew perfectly well there was not.

Yet we also love. The words we speak in haste are forgiven, and a hug follows. But do we forgive ourselves? So rarely do we ask this question, yet it's huge. Because to live without forgiveness—without letting ourselves off the hook—is not living at all. The difficulty we have in forgiving ourselves is bound up with our sense of shame.

Shame paralyzes. Shame puts a gag over our hearts and stops up all the words of love and praise that our families need. Shame causes us to brace, as though we were heading into an accident. We treat our lives like hide-and-seek, hoping no one will ever find us and reveal our shame. And if we are found, up go our fists—fight or flight. Hiding is painful. It's a sort of *dis-ease* of the soul.

To begin to throw off the chains of shame, we must look at ourselves with love. One of life's paradoxes is that we need to embrace our whole selves so that we can cease to see the "imperfections" in others. Today's exercises will help you reflect on this.

Rooibos Tea

Made from the oxidized leaves of a member of the pea family, rooibos tea is naturally caffeine free. An antioxidant, it helps promote digestion, boosts the immune system, and relieves allergies, asthma, and upset stomach. It also contains a number of minerals, including calcium.

As much as any other product of South Africa, rooibos has brought the indigenous black and the immigrant white populations together. This was so from the moment European immigrants first appreciated the therapeutic and pleasurable use the Khoisan people had for the leaves of the *Aspalathus linearis* bush to its far more recent popularization around the world—thanks in part to businesses committed to investing in social justice. To cite an outstanding example, the Heiveld Cooperative (easily found online) has sold fair-trade organic tea since 2000. Its integrated board offers a model for that unfinished project: the full reconciliation of South Africa's long balkanized communities. What better tea could there be for a day devoted to forgiveness?

You can brew rooibos just as you do conventional tea, but be sure to let it steep at least five minutes, as its health effects increase the longer the leaves remain in contact with water.

If you use a teabag, pay special attention to the change in color—the red can be quite lovely. To see what happens to a tea as it steeps, you'll want either a cup with a pure white interior or one made of colorless glass. Have you seen the effect sunlight can have as it passes through a glass full of scarlet tea?

Take a few moments to notice the changes in your cup. Notice your mind's reaction. Are you enjoying this experience? Now notice the aroma. Does it remind you of something? Taste the tea. How does your body respond? You might label your reactions, and then let them pass. As you like. Nothing is necessary at this moment. There is no good and bad.

Mandala Artwork

As you settle into creating this mandala, summon to mind all the little events (and there may be some large ones) for which you would like to be forgiven. Choose colors that match the events, relying on your intuitive association of certain emotions with specific colors. Think back on the events, and as each of these stories unfolds, and the color is laid down on paper, forgive yourself. You need no other person or higher being for forgiveness. You are your only judge.

When you're done, take a moment to appreciate the two mandalas you've colored: today's and yesterday's. No criticism, not even so-called constructive criticism, is allowed. Notice your color choices and how the light changes things. Would you like to put one on the wall to look at in order to support meditation?

Movement

Let's begin by warming up, slowly. First, you'll repeat the movements you learned on day 1, and then we'll combine them with today's new poses. These are the early movements of a moon salutation.

WARM UP: CHILD'S POSE; EXTENDED CHILD'S POSE; ALL FOURS

Be sure to listen for any information your body is communicating to you at the beginning of your practice.

Now let's move on to our new movements.

ALL FOURS; FACE DOWN; ALL FOURS

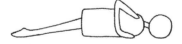

All Fours

Face Down

All Fours

ALL FOURS

Arms should be directly under your shoulders.
Your weight is distributed evenly between hands and knees.

Now, take a few breaths while on your hands and knees. Be sure to reignite the energy in your hands and their connection to the ground, doing the same for the tops of your feet. Be sure your arms are under your shoulders, providing good support.

Imagine energy coming up your arms, into your relaxed shoulders, and an equal amount of energy going back down your arms into your hands. Allow your shoulders to roll away from your ears and release down your back. Your face should be soft, relaxed, at rest. What is your mind doing? Just notice, no need to judge.

FACE DOWN

On an exhale, lower your upper body down to the ground.
Your chest is on the ground, legs stretched out long.
Forehead and nose are touching the ground.
Hands with palms flat are on either side of your chest.

Without losing the connection you've made to the ground with your hands and the tops of your feet, allow the entire core of your body to soften. Breathe freely. Invite the ground to hold you. Soften every joint and muscle. Surrender.

ALL FOURS

On an exhale, rise back onto all fours.

You have been in this pose several times now. Does it feel more familiar now? Repeat this *ulola*, or series of postures, five times—or more, if you like. This is a simple move. All the moves you will do with me are simple and basic. Use this time as an opportunity to pay attention to what your body and mind are saying in movement. As these moves become more familiar, your mind will settle and the wisdom of your body will be better heard.

Now connect this three-part ulola—all fours, face down, all fours—with yesterday's series of postures, and repeat all of them in order: extended child's pose, all fours, and face down. Go through these moves five times. (As our list of yoga poses builds, use the pull out guide in the back of this book to guide you.)

Keep your mind soft. Listen to your body. What is it saying? Let your body—not your mind—tell you when you are done.

Did any frustration arise in reaction to these poses? Were you concerned that you might have messed them up? Any way you did the poses is correct.

Interlude

Forgiving Myself

Nearly two decades ago, I traveled to Washington, DC, with a group of fifteen- and sixteen-year-olds—fifty of them in all. They were my students, and I hoped to show them the District and some of the places and objects that figure so prominently in our nation's history. Since we were coming from California, the highlight was going to be a meeting with Senator Dianne Feinstein. We landed at the peak of the cherry blossoms—an auspicious beginning.

Within twenty-four hours, the two other teachers who'd made the trip were out of commission. A fractured molar and a bad fall, and it was just me with all those students. I loved it. I felt free from the judgment of the other teachers and was able to relax and bond with a group I already knew quite well. Our days rushed by. We saw all the sights, crying and laughing along the way. On the final day, the plan was to meet the senator. I was both excited and nervous.

Before heading to Ms. Feinstein's office, we ate lunch at the Old Post Office Pavilion, near the Mall. Then we headed to the bus we'd chartered. Once we'd boarded, I did my usual head count: we were short two students: two intelligent and politically savvy girls named Tira and Louise. I looked everywhere and had them paged over the post office PA system. Nothing. The sure signs of anxiety surged into my body. Was this really happening? Were these inconsiderate kids going to make us miss our appointment?

When I finally thought to look in the bathroom, there they were, gaily chatting away. I stood there, the furious adult confronting two truants. One look at me, and they fell silent. The smiles dropped from their faces. I hissed, "*Who* do you think you are?" No answer.

We missed the meeting with Senator Feinstein, but a congressman, taking pity on these Californians so far from home, consented to talk with us for a few minutes. The students squirmed through it, asking no questions, desperately longing for it to be over; I had managed to infect them with my own misery.

Let's rewind to the moment in that bathroom. What was it I said, exactly? *Who do you think you are?* In a certain tone of voice, that might be an invitation to reflect on one's identity. I spoke loudly, shrilly. I was going after who they were, not what they did. I treated them as though they were bad people, when in fact they are great people. I targeted their very souls, leaving them no way to say they were sorry or to make things right.

Can you ask to be forgiven for being a bad person? No, but you can ask for forgiveness for acting thoughtlessly. I wish I'd said, "I am upset because you weren't on time for the bus. Your classmates are all waiting for you." But I didn't; I shamed them. No teacher should act as I did, and I've been upset with myself for years. So I guess it is time to forgive myself and understand my motives.

I went after Tira and Louise the way I did because back then I didn't distinguish well enough between my actions and myself. When my actions were unskillful, as they were that afternoon, I would draw conclusions about my inner being: *I am a "bad" person because a "good" person would not have acted that way.* This made me feel unworthy as a person, triggering deep shame about who I was. I transferred this shame to my students; I treated those two wonderful girls the way I treated myself. But now I can ask for that shame back, and I can heal it. I can forgive myself.

We've all done things we regret, things we feel shame about. Shame and regret fester within us, keeping us from being a true friend to ourselves and others. (For parents, this can be disastrous. If we want to express love, we'd be better off turning inward first, uncovering and addressing our old wounds, the ones we inflicted on ourselves, before transferring our shame to our children.)

How can we move beyond unhealthy shame and regret? To introduce one way of healing, I'll call on an ancient meditation: the forgiveness meditation.

Meditation: Forgiveness

When I was first introduced to the forgiveness meditation many years ago, it showed me how critical I was of myself and others. As time went on, and I became more self-aware—more mindful—I found myself reaching for the words of the meditation when I heard myself speaking critically. But too often, I grew flustered and failed to summon the precious verses. So I wrote them down on an index card that I keep in my bag to this day, though the simple phrases now spill easily from my lips. I still use these phrases. Just the other day, when I thought my son was not responding respectfully to the e-mails of his friend, something that drew some criticism from me, I quickly forgave myself, an act that changed the energy between my child and me. This made possible a balanced conversation about what had happened.

To start this meditation, assume a comfortable position, and bring your attention to your breath, not controlling it but observing the natural ebb and flow of exhalation, inhalation. Sit for a few moments, drop into your heart, and simply be with yourself.

While allowing your body to be upright, keep your heart soft and open to the possibilities that forgiveness sets before you.

Let us begin by asking for forgiveness for what we have done to others. This may have been an unkind comment, a selfish act, or a betrayal. It may be that we didn't offer what we could have: a steadying hand, a consoling comment, a job, some money. Allow your thoughts to move over the people you've hurt and ignored. As each memory arises, extend yourself forgiveness.

> I openly grant myself forgiveness.
> I hold myself in mercy and compassion.

Repeat this phrase aloud for each occasion that swims into your mind's eye. Say it as many times as is necessary.

Let's continue shedding the pain we've caused ourselves. To cast off the baggage you've borne for so long, think of the ways you blame yourself, the hurt you do by refusing to forget failings large and small. The time has come to let go of all the ways you've brought pain and harm to yourself, knowingly and unknowingly, in words and actions.

> I openly grant myself forgiveness.
> I extend to myself mercy and compassion.

Repeat these words as many times as necessary. You deserve to be forgiven; we all do. It is this forgiveness that will allow your heart to open.

And now, forgive those who have harmed and hurt you by what they have done and what they have not done. These people reacted due to their own fear and suffering, knowingly or unknowingly. Grant them your forgiveness. Doing so will release the anger that imprisons you, and with it the pain and suffering you cause yourself and those you love.

> I openly grant you my forgiveness.
> I extend to you mercy and compassion, to the extent I can at this time.

It may not be time to let go of all the hurt you feel at this moment, but release the hurt that you can. Over time—days and weeks, months, and years—you will continue to release more and more of the hurt you carry. Carrying that hurt only harms you. There is no fun in living with a closed heart.

Journal Activity: Shame versus Guilt

Give some thought to what guilt is. Write a definition or a few thoughts below.

_____

_____

_____

Give some thought to what shame is. Set down a definition or some thoughts below.

_____

_____

_____

Sit in a comfortable position and think of a time when you experienced shame. How would you then have completed the following sentence?

"I am bad because I _____."

Take the time to revive that feeling of shame. Feel and see the emotions that run through you. Write some thoughts or draw some images below.

Now, take the exact same event and think about it in slightly different terms. The key is the following sentence. "I made a mistake when I _____." (This is your edited event.)

Take time to try to walk through the emotions that come to you as you reflect on the event through this edited perspective. When you have done so, use the space below to write down how it was different from the first experience.

_____

_____

_____

A time will come when once again you make a mistake or do something you are unhappy with or embarrassed by. When that happens, what simple change can you make to your inner dialogue? You will discover that feeling shame or guilt is a choice; it does not have to play out identically every time you stumble. Write your thoughts below.

_____

_____

_____

It may seem like a fine point, but I want to insist that there is a crucial difference between shame and guilt. It's the difference between "I am bad" and "I did something bad." Guilt means, "I made a mistake." Shame too often means, "I am a mistake." If you learn to be more loving of yourself, you'll avoid clubbing yourself over the head with either emotion. Only then can you see others in a more compassionate light.

Closure

Today you've been thinking about what it means to feel shame and what it means to forgive. My experience working with many different groups has taught me that nothing can be more crippling to the ties between two people—business associates, brother and sister, married partners, a parent and child—than a sense of wrong that goes unacknowledged. Saying, "I'm sorry," can make a huge change, but do not wait for it. Instead, offer forgiveness freely.

In today's interlude, I proposed a very simple formula that can be used for forgiveness. It is directed within—your heart speaking to itself. Tomorrow we will begin to see what happens next, as we look at other tools to guide you in healing yourself.

3

Looking within
to Heal

From early in life, we learn to mourn. We bury even the tiniest pets, often with a prayer, and some of the year's changes, especially the end of summer, are marked with what soon becomes a formula for grief. A ruined shirt, a game cut short, a painting faded in the sun, the disappearance of the last piece of cake—all these provoke regrets, even tears.

To be a parent is to teach a child how to express joy and suffering, to participate in an old cycle you yourself went through many times. So when that child packs a suitcase and heads for the door, why is the parent the only one crying? That inequity can be a bit disheartening for the parent— and for the child as well, though in different ways. But grief is learned, and a parent has far more experience with partings than a teenager has. Why wish any premature sadness on an adored one?

Today we'll look at how to handle buried sadness, including some of the clues that show where it lies, and we'll learn to both acknowledge and begin to heal the wounds life leaves on our hearts.

Ginger Tea

Worlds away from the teas that set you abuzz with caffeine, ginger tea soothes nerves and nausea, aids in digestion, enhances appetite, eases inflammation of the joints, fights coughs and colds, improves blood circulation, strengthens your immune system, and relieves stress.

Some of the world's oldest civilizations—China, India, Greece—prized the healing properties of this root (Egyptians preferred garlic), so it's the perfect sip as we begin a day devoted to the theme of curing yourself of emotional wounds.

One of the best ways to make a ginger infusion is the simplest. Wash a plump, fresh knob of organic ginger root. Slice it thinly, put it in a glass measuring cup, pour boiling water over it, steep for ten minutes, and then strain and drink. You may want to add a teaspoon of honey and a tablespoon of fresh lemon juice.

This tea is energizing. So after finishing the cup, pay special attention to your energy level. After about twenty minutes, you might notice an increase in heart rate and overall energy. Take some time to pay close attention to your body's reaction to this tea. Do you sense any change? If so—or if not—how do you feel about this realization? Spend some time noticing your feelings about the tea.

Mandala Artwork

Take a moment to imagine your physical body. Recall the cuts and bruises of childhood and the marks they left. Recall the emotional pains of life, hurt feelings, loneliness, and harsh words and locate their "marks" on your body. Touch all these spots tenderly. After a few breaths, open to the possibility of embracing and loving each and every part of you, scarred and unscarred.

Color this mandala to show appreciation for the strength, agility, intelligence, and beauty of your body. If you are struggling to love a particular part of your physical self, touch those feelings gently and take your time filling in your mandala with a special color that represents this tender piece of you. In time, and with an open heart, you will see the beauty in every single part of you.

Movement

Begin by moving through the postures from days 1 and 2.

CHILD'S POSE; EXTENDED CHILD'S POSE; ALL
FOURS; FACE DOWN; ALL FOURS

Now let's move onto our new movements.

ALL FOURS; DOWN DOG WITH LEGS BENT; ALL FOURS

All Fours

Down Dog With Legs Bent

All Fours

Take a few breaths here, and notice your body's reaction to the postures.

ALL FOURS

Balance your weight between hands and knees.

While on your hands and knees, reconnect your hands and the tops of your feet to the earth. Breathe into this familiar pose.

DOWN DOG WITH LEGS BENT

Turn your toes under and then push up into down-facing dog.
Your knees are softly bent to nourish your lower back.
Rise high on the balls of your feet.
Completely relax your neck!

Allow your shoulders to release back and down. Just notice your mind. How is it responding to this first pose off the floor? Are your knees bent? They should be bent to support your lower back. Is your neck completely relaxed? Is your reaction neutral, pleasant, or unpleasant? Just notice. No need to judge.

ALL FOURS

Gently return to your hands and knees.
Keep all joints soft.

Repeat this series of movements five times or more. Each repetition will be a little different. It will always be a bit different. You are never exactly the same as you were at any moment in the past.

Now connect all the poses, moving through the postures slowly and with attention. Repeat all of the poses from day 1 through today until your body announces that you're finished. (Remember that there is a guide in the back of this book with all the movements pictured.) Let this come from your body, not your mind. Watch this dance between mind and body. Be curious about it.

Interlude

Finding Your Grief

The story that follows prompted the book you are holding. I heard it while sitting in a kitchen and watching a fifty-year-old woman (my sister-in-law, Liane) arrange a family photo album. Liane and my brother, Markus, have two boys: Xander and Guy. I already knew, from various accounts, that the process of applying to colleges had been trying, not just for Xander but for the whole family. Completing the essays, gathering the recommendations, and rounding out extracurricular activities had led to many tense moments and arguments and emotional distance. But on that day, a year after Xander had left for college, I heard Liane's account for the first time.

I've always been deeply impressed by my sister-in-law. A calming presence at the pivot of the very male family, she filters and recasts the words slung between three guys who have a ballplayer's approach to communication. Liane's color commentary helps them hear each other, listen, and bond. Her timing is stunning, and she possesses the rare skill of seeing humor in situations without trivializing them. But while she so brilliantly mediated, she was neglecting her own emotions.

The time since Xander's departure had been far more painful than the struggle to get him through the application process. Liane explained that the switch was abrupt: he very quickly struck out on an independent life at school. New friends, new ideas, new responsibilities—they absorbed and enchanted him. He rarely called. Liane has a full life—a career, friends, Markus, and Guy—but she also had an empty room upstairs where her son no longer slept. She had a breakfast table with an empty chair. Even her role of mediator in the ballplayers' talk felt different. Everything had changed.

She spoke of regret—of the things she had wanted to do while her family was all together. She spent hours assembling albums of photographs taken on past family trips and editing home videos. She reread Xander's favorite books, the ones they used to talk about. She mourned. She felt her loss. She wept.

I sat and listened. What was there to say?

Mourning is good. Even sadness is good. In taking the time to create these photo albums, Liane acted mindfully. She gave herself the time she needed, which allowed her to embrace this change in her family. This book introduces you to a number of practices centered on mindfulness to support your family's experience at this time of transition. There is a voice within each of us that knows what to do. Mindfulness creates ease and calm, allowing this voice to be heard.

Meditation: Wisdom Resides Within

This meditation was introduced to me by my tai chi instructor. He simply offered it to his students one day before our usual morning class. This was in 1986. It is as meaningful today as it was back then.

Find yourself in your usual meditation position. Take a few moments to ground and to feel connected with the earth. Allow your breath to be your focus. Be curious about this breath, as though you were noticing it for the first time. Settle in, drop down into your heart, and simply be here, right now.

Once you have grounded, invite your memory to recall a time when you were in a position that you found very difficult, a time when you were struggling with a person or a situation. Allow the images and the memories of this event to flood your mind. Sit and feel how your body responds to this memory. Notice what feelings this event brings up. Sit for a few minutes and allow any sensations to show themselves. Invite the details of this event to emerge. Imagine the location, the weather, the furniture, a scent.

Now, imagine yourself in that location. To one side is a tall oak door you had not previously noticed. It has a heavy, brass doorknob. Reach for that doorknob, twist it, and open the door. There you find an inspirational figure: Jesus Christ, Guan Yin, Elijah, Buddha, the Triple Goddess, Mohammed, or someone else entirely. It's someone that you trust to do the right thing in difficult situations. He or she invites you to change identities. You become her, and she becomes you. As you watch, she passes through the door and enters the location where your difficult event took place. Everything that happened to you now happens to her, except that her reactions set her apart. You hear what she says. You see what she does. You see the result and the changes that occur under her care.

When she is done, she walks back to you, and again you trade places. She hands you a small gift. You thank her, with deep and profound gratitude.

You open the gift. It is just perfect.

Sit a while longer and note any feelings this meditation brings up. Are the feelings pleasant, unpleasant, or neutral?

Now bow deeply to the wisdom that resides within you. Bow deeply to the care that you are taking with yourself. Bow to the trust you have in yourself.

Journal Activity: Healing Wounds

As you carry out this activity, you will be identifying some of the wounds you harbor then opening pathways to begin to heal. You can use this activity over and over again, turning to it every time you experience reactivity to a situation. Whenever you have a strong emotional reaction—anger, pride, withdrawal—whenever you cry, tremble, or feel a dark mood overwhelm you, an emotional wound has been touched. This reaction is a gift, the key to your internal world. This exercise is designed to help you turn the key. In time and with practice, you will better understand your reaction and what triggers it.

For example, I used to get angry at my husband when I thought he was paying too much attention to our dog, a rather charming mutt named Curly. After some searching and meditating, I realized that the vulnerability my husband shows Curly reminded me of another man in my life. When I was young, nothing scared me more than the rare glimpses I caught of my father's weak spots, those points on the map of his soul where shifting plates and treacherous currents overlapped. Seeing my father in my husband, really one of the most natural things in life, terrified me. When I join others in this exercise, we often realize something we never suspected.

Sit quietly in your meditation position and recall an event that triggered strong negative emotions. Examples include an argument, having your feelings hurt, or being badly frightened. Take some time to remember the event and briefly describe it below.

_____

_____

_____

What feelings arise in response to this event?

_____

_____

_____

Continue to sit in your meditation position, and invite your mind to calm. Allow your attention to go inward. Take some breaths, and feel your body.

Do you feel sensations in your body that are associated with the feelings you listed above? If yes, use the diagram below to locate them. Mark an *X* where you feel the strongest sensation. If you do not have an identifiable physical sensation, place an *X* in the area of the heart.

Set a timer for ten minutes. Focus your mind's eye on the area of your body where you marked an *X* above. Open to feeling this area of your body in a new way. Your mind will probably wander, because it does not like to sit with things that are uncomfortable. If so, just bring your attention back to the feeling in your body. Just focus on this vibration, pain, heaviness, warmth, nothingness—whatever the sensation may be. Just stay with it. Just watch it with curiosity. What is it doing? Is it moving? Is it pulsing? Do you associate a color with it? Which color? Is nothing happening? Just stay open to the possibility of surrender.

When your timer goes off, answer the questions below. (You may not be able to answer all of them.)

Describe any sensations you felt, such as strong, weak, tingling, irritation, vibration, heat, and pain. Take your time to find a way to describe the feeling, even if it seems like you felt nothing.

_____

_____

_____

Was it difficult or easy for your mind to focus on this area of your body? Why?

_____

_____

_____

Did any images or words come to mind while you were focusing on this area of your body? Write or draw them here.

What is your interpretation of these words or images?

_____

_____

_____

If your mind wandered and you were able to bring your focus back to the physical sensation in your body, what skill allowed you to refocus? If you are unsure, just use the space below to describe what you did, such as here: "When I realized my mind wandered from my meditation, I simply went back to the heaviness in my chest and focused on it."

_____

_____

_____

Give some thought to why you found your way to this area of your body. There may be no obvious answer. This is just an inquiry. Listen to your body. Does it have any other information for you?

_____

_____

_____

If you did this activity again, what would you change to make it a more powerful experience?

_____

_____

_____

I invite you to use this exercise over and over again, whenever your emotions crowd in on you. Simply feel your body's response to the world around you. Sit and feel your reaction to pleasure, joy, and sadness. This activity nurtures the growing respect you have for the wisdom of your body. It knows so much. All we need to do is listen and surrender to our own wisdom.

Closure

· ·

The heart stores feelings throughout the body. We feel a twinge in the shoulder when we recall a job that nearly sunk us. Isn't that where that difficult boss used to place her hand, even as she ladled on the abuse? Often, the connection is less transparent but no less real. In your journal activity, you pinned down the location of one of those psychic wounds, a first step toward healing it. My message is the same here as elsewhere: few lessons are as important as learning to listen to the body, something modern life often discourages.

People cope with pain in many ways, and many therapies help. An important insight for many who suffer from chronic pain is that some part of them insists that the misery is deserved; their emotions are summoning the pain as a kind of punishment. Seeing that we often are the ones causing the pain is a first step to finding a treatment that makes sense. You'll know your solution when you find it. Tomorrow we'll turn from reflections on past hurts to a forward-facing attitude.

DAY

4

Looking Forward

If we did not have our attention fixed on the world around us, just imagine the consequences. Still, we manage to spend a lot of time dwelling on the past, frozen in thousands of photographs of birthday parties, camping trips, bat mitzvahs, first communions, and so on. The past is a place we go when the present doesn't seem to be working out. But if we want to change our present, we need to see that the problems we encounter today generally have their sources in the past. Yet if we carefully look at our past, it is full of clues that can help us see patterns. Seeing these patterns begins our healing. But our future is created right now, at this present moment. To do this mindfully, our past needs to be released. Abundant love of ourselves, of each other, and of nature invites more love. Can you imagine the possibilities?

To move beyond the habits handed to us by our parents and other influential figures, we discover a self that has little to do with heredity, imprinting, and coercion. If we live mindfully, we learn to avoid making our children, or our future children, in our own image. They prove remarkably skillful at fashioning themselves.

Masala Chai

Chai, a Sanskrit word traceable to the Chinese word *cha,* means nothing other than "tea." Masala chai, or "spiced tea," a specialty of India now drunk wherever Indian food is found, is a blend of black tea, milk, ginger, green cardamom, and some or all of the following: clove, cinnamon, black pepper, nutmeg, fennel, and star anise. Chai is believed to improve cardiovascular health, increase memory, and relax the central nervous system.

In India, preparing masala chai means boiling black tea leaves (Assam works well) with whole spices, straining the fragrant result, and then adding a bit of buffalo milk. You may prefer loose tea or a teabag stuffed with organic spices and tea leaves. While milk of some kind is essential, it's up to you to choose soy, dairy, or condensed. Steep until it reaches the desired strength. Since it is based on true tea, there is plenty of caffeine in most versions, although decaffeinated is available. Many people like their chai quite sweet; I simply add a teaspoon of honey to my cup.

Sit for a few moments while holding your cup of chai. The spices used are all categorized by Ayurvedic practitioners as warming (in contrast to spearmint tea, which is cooling) and are best enjoyed when you need soothing. As masala chai is thought to bring balance to critical thinking as well as to the senses, it is appropriate for this day, which will call on your rational mind more than any other day.

Now sniff your cup of tea, noticing the aroma and its impact on your body. As you sip, do you sense your mind settling into a greater balance?

Mandala Artwork

As we move forward from our *heart*, allow the colors of love—love of people, places, animals, and yourself—to flood your mind. Now color your mandala to reflect this possibility. Ask yourself why you chose a particular color. How curious! When you are done notice which color you used the most. Which color did you use the least? Did you choose a color for yourself? Amazing!

Movement

Begin by moving through the postures from days 1, 2, and 3.

CHILD'S POSE; EXTENDED CHILD'S POSE; ALL FOURS; FACE
DOWN; ALL FOURS; DOWN DOG LEGS BENT; ALL FOURS

Now let's move on to today's poses.

DOWN DOG; FORWARD FOLD; FINGERTIPS

Down Dog With Legs Bent

Forward Fold

Finger Tips

Do you feel any changes to your breath? What, if any, are the impacts of those changes on your mind?

DOWN DOG

Your knees are bent.
Rest high on the balls of your feet.
Your weight is distributed evenly between hands and feet.
Keep knees softly bent to nourish your lower back.
Completely relax you neck.

Take a moment to find your center and breathe into it. Allow your belly to soften even more. This pose is familiar now. How does that resonate with you?

FORWARD FOLD

Step forward to your hands.
Keep your feet parallel with each other, hip width apart.
Your palms are flat on the floor.
Knees bent.
Keep your neck relaxed.

You are in a forward bend. Allow your head to be completely relaxed, and allow your face to soften. Keep your knees bent to protect your lower back. Notice any new sensations in your body and in your mind.

FINGERTIPS

Straighten your spine, rising onto your fingertips.
Look down at your hands.
Keep your knees bent.

Your legs stay bent and your abdomen soft. Allow your back to adopt a neutral shape so there is a softness in your lower back. Keep the front of your body relaxed. Maintain your connection with the ground through the tips of your fingers and the soles of your feet. Allow your arms to connect to your relaxed shoulders. Relax your shoulders gently away from your ears to allow your upper back to open and release anything that you might be holding there.

Place your palms back on the ground and step back to down-facing dog. Repeat this five times. Now connect all of the poses you've learned so far. Repeat the entire sequence five times or more. All the while, as you move through the ulola, listen to yourself; hear yourself. What emotions arise in this gentle upside-down position? How is your mind reacting? Was this ever a favorite position of yours?

Interlude

The Beliefs of Others

The beliefs of others are all around us, and it is a challenge to wade through all of these opinions and ideas and be clear about which ones are ours. This story illustrates just how confusing these messages can be.

A loud and determined knock interrupted my class. We all fell silent, turned toward the door, and held our breath. The door opened a bit, and a student named Merche peeked in. The bang on the door, the timid look—here was a student torn between two very different impulses. She asked to talk to me in the hall. My students wordlessly and approvingly ushered me out. They obviously knew what was going on.

The moment I'd closed the classroom door, Merche launched into her confession. The words poured out. Sex … condom … ripped … AIDS … death. I knew Merche and her boyfriend Francisco well—both had been my students. I was hardly surprised to hear that they'd had sex the night before—her first time. And as I would have expected of two intelligent, young people, they had used a condom. But this frightened girl thought it had ripped. She was far from Francisco's first sex partner. Had she contracted HIV? Spinning out of control, breathing quickly, here was the face of panic.

Leaving my students to carry on by themselves, I led her down the hall. In my office, Merche broke down again, this time sobbing uncontrollably. She flopped to the ground, unable to speak. I put my arms around her, and there we sat, saying nothing.

Once she was able to talk, Merche blurted out that she deserved to get HIV. That was the price one paid for sex. Hmm. I had twenty minutes before my next class, so I suggested a walk. A half-block had gone by when I broke the silence. "Your life is changing. You want a deeper, more intimate relationship with Francisco. How are you feeling about this decision?"

Sometimes the most obvious questions are the best ones. Within a couple of minutes, I learned that Merche's mother opposed sex before marriage. And didn't sex strip away innocence, pushing you into the adult world, where sex is used to manipulate and control? Hadn't Merche pushed herself outside the circle of her loved ones?

When I gently suggested that she might talk to her mother about all of this, Merche gave me a look that completed the picture. She was scared that she would lose her mother's love. Then she really would be alone—completely alone. This would be her worst nightmare realized.

As we headed back, I asked Merche a question. "You just said so much about sex and the loss of innocence and the bad world it pushes you into. Are these *your* beliefs?" Merche said nothing, but I could see I'd struck a chord. We hugged and I went to my next class.

Over the subsequent months, Merche and I spoke again several times. She moved from the dread and panic of our initial conversations to more mindful assessments and realizations about what had happened. She even laughed when I reminded her that she'd equated losing her virginity with death. Most important of all, though, Merche took ownership of what had transpired, situating it in a set of values that were her own. And she did talk with her mother, finding a middle ground where a conversation was possible. Merche still had issues, but they were issues she could evaluate and address on her own terms. When all the medical tests turned out negative, Merche was not just relieved but ready to move forward in her relationship with Francisco.

When I think about Merche, a decade later, I think about the ways in which we are affected by the statements of our parents, the opinions of our friends, and the values of our communities. Unthinkingly, we make these ideas our own, only to find ourselves at odds with them later.

You may have seen this process in action quite recently with your own family. Some people come to fear that if they don't abide by the views of their loved ones they will find themselves alone. But their loved ones offer a range of views, and soon it proves impossible to satisfy every constituency. Also, *even when the views of others are good and valuable, they still come from outside. We need to make them our own.* Mindful reflection and mindful practice can be a big help in this process.

Meditation: Walking

This meditation taught me how to bring mindfulness into my daily life. I practice it often and with great joy because it allows me to be mindful while walking, navigating obstacles like steps, judging my balance, directing my gaze, and taking in scenery. Nothing is too trivial to escape the benefits of this meditation. Just writing about it brings a smile to my face.

To begin, find an area in which you can take about ten steps without worrying about any obstacles. Either indoors or out will work. Set a timer for ten minutes to start. Now, take those ten steps, turn, and retrace your steps. Use the following words to guide you: "Lifting, swinging, touching down." This refers to the movement of your foot lifting off the floor, swinging forward, and then touching down on the ground. You can repeat this phrase as many times as is helpful. Your attention is focused on the movement. Continue until you've used up your ten minutes.

This meditation is about going forward without arriving. In this instance, walking is not a means to an end. The focus of your walk is the walking itself. When your mind wanders, come back to your breath, your walking steps, or to the mantra "Lifting, swinging, touching down." To add a walking meditation to your repertoire is to advance toward bringing more mindfulness to everyday moments. Smile with me at the simplicity of it.

Journal Activity: Who Else Am I?

In the box below, list seven of your mother's best qualities.

In the box below, list seven of your father's best qualities.

Note: use the list of qualities at the end of this section only if necessary.

Box A

Box B

In the box below, list seven of your mother's worst qualities.

Box C

In the box below, list seven of your father's worst qualities.

Box D

In the box below, list the seven characteristics you like most about yourself.

Box E

In the box below, list the seven characteristics you like least about yourself.

Box F

Do some of the characteristics listed in Boxes E and F match some of those listed in Boxes A, B, C, and D? Circle them, and then list them below. This is a list of characteristics you share with your parents.

Box G (Shared Qualities)

Look at the qualities listed in box G. Take a few moments to think about the qualities you share with your parents, both good and bad. Is it possible that some of these qualities are not truly yours and you are just borrowing them from your parents? Put the words from box G in the sentences below.

Am I truly _____, or is this a quality my parents wanted me to have?

Am I truly _____, or is this my parents' characteristic?

Was I born _____, or did I adopt it from my parents or someone else?

I don't want to be _____. Is it possible that I'm not?

As you uncover the qualities that are not truly your own, you can give them away. Simply say, "I give this back to the universe to heal myself, those I love, and the entire planet."

Which of your characteristics listed in boxes E and F were left uncircled? These are your qualities, those that you do not share with your parents. List them below.

Box H (The True Me)

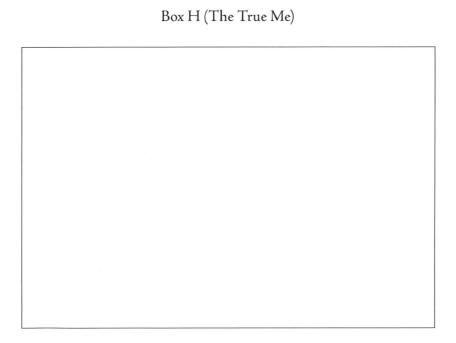

Now take a close look at the qualities listed in box H. Ask yourself if all really apply to you. Where did they come from? Just take some time to wonder and question something you haven't questioned before. Just be curious about it. Get to know yourself a little better.

Who Else Am I? A List of Traits

Moody	Funny	Touchy	Honest
Bold	Kind	Annoyed	Jealous
Open-minded	Angry	Shy	Dishonest
Safe	Available	Thrifty	Bossy
Playful	Spiritual	Critical	Childlike
Cautious	Playful	Brutal	Fragile
Inappropriate	Unpredictable	Spontaneous	Stingy
Creative	Caring	Sincere	Tolerant
Generous	Wise	Productive	Lazy
Rough	Alert	Courageous	Attacking
Connected	Depressed	Agreeable	Arrogant
Tense	Dependable	Inflexible	Stable
Crafty	Boring	Sincere	Sad
Grumpy	Wise	Afraid	Shy
Helpful	Anxious	Creative	Respectful
Hardworking	Fair	Polite	Reliable
Calm	Quiet	Emotionally Unavailable	Present
Judgmental	Curious	Fearful	Gullible

Closure

Merche's experience showed me just how paralyzing the parent-child link can be when it goes wrong, but it also proved just how resourceful and wise a teenager can be when given a chance to speak with her own voice. Distinguishing your intrinsic nature from the bits and pieces that you acquire from others can liberate you from internal turmoil. In fact, making this distinction is the essence of mindfulness. Living mindfully in this way allows our true self to grow.

A family can grow together as long as its members keep their hearts open to one another, accepting that each must be a separate individual.

DAY

5

Healing Together

Early in this book, I declared that love was the answer. And while love has come up on each of the last four days, today it is central. Some groundwork needed to be done before we could unleash the power of love. We needed to see that it is possible to better understand who we were, and possible to forgive ourselves and others, so that we could see ourselves as fully worthy of love. We needed to accept that we are what we make ourselves, that we can never be happy relying on the opinions of others. The moments in these past four days are just the beginning. Now I want to take this one step further—to show how the qualities that we react to most in others may be those we possess ourselves. So as we heal, our compassion for others will grow and that invites them to heal. We can heal together.

All of this comes at a price, and moving on may be a difficult process, even painful. Such pain itself has no value, and I'd never wish it on anyone, but it's essential. In this case, pain reminds you of all the times love failed to win the day, of all the times that your essential identity was buried under someone else's suffering. And allowing that pain to show itself means growth. Yet we must eventually come to the deep truth that we are more than our pain. This realization sets us free, and it is available to all of us.

Things are changing. Change with them. Whenever there is upheaval in your family, you will need to temper the impulse to continue as things have always been. Have patience and take pride in the person you are and the transitions you are all embracing.

Green Tea

Although green tea has always been more popular in China and Japan than black tea (an extra step in processing triggers oxidation, turning green leaves black), Americans have only recently embraced green tea because of its health benefits. Mildly caffeinated, green tea is loaded with antioxidants, improves digestion and memory, wards off dementia, and may lower cholesterol. Its effectiveness in zapping oral bacteria, viral hepatitis, and arthritis connects it to our day of healing.

There are hundreds of different green teas. Among the most famous are China's longjing, bilochun, and jasmine and Japan's sencha and matcha. Other countries, such as Sri Lanka and India, also make fine green teas. Seek out something you haven't tried before.

Steep your green tea for a few minutes until it reaches the desired strength. As you hold your warm cup and sip, what areas of your body does the drink touch, open, or affect? What are your feet, hands, and back saying about this experience? Think about the connection between your hands and shoulders. If your mind wanders off, come back to the aroma and to your breath, allowing a reconnection with your body.

Mandala Artwork

This mandala is inviting you to add more of yourself. Take time now to add your favorite shapes. Reach beyond the boundaries of the form and of your imagination. Act from your heart alone, not your mind. Open deeply to the beauty that resides within you right now, and color this mandala as a gift just for you.

Movement

Begin by moving through the postures from days 1, 2, 3, and 4.

CHILD'S POSE; EXTENDED CHILD'S POSE; ALL FOURS;
FACE DOWN; ALL FOURS; DOWN DOG LEGS BENT; ALL FOURS;
DOWN DOG LEGS BENT; FORWARD FOLD; FINGERTIPS

Now let's move to our final series of movements.

FORWARD BEND ON FINGERTIPS; CHAIR POSE; MOUNTAIN POSE

Finger Tips

Chair Pose

Mountain Pose

As you add the last poses of moon salutation, how do you feel? Bored, interested, curious? Everything is welcome. Just notice, without judgment.

FORWARD BEND ON FINGERTIPS

Your knees are bent.
Lower your gaze.
Keep your feet and hands active and alive.
You are in a forward fold position.

With knees bent and head relaxed, rise so that your fingertips are barely resting on the earth and your spine unfolds. On an exhale, bend your knees a little more and raise your hands and arms up and forward. Keep your weight evenly balanced in your feet. Be sure to ground into the earth through your feet. Keep your arms active and connected to your relaxed shoulders.

CHAIR POSE

Raise your arms toward the sky.
Bend your knees a bit more.
Ground your feet to support your lower back.
Maintain the soft curve in your lower spine.

From here, ground through your feet, keeping your toes free to move, and straighten your legs, while lowering your arms to rise into mountain pose.

MOUNTAIN POSE

Push through your entire foot to straighten up.
Find your center.
Relax your arms at your sides.
Ground through your feet.
Keep your hands active and participating.

Take some breaths here. For the first time in this series of ulolas, you are standing. Notice how your arms feel next to your body. Notice your breath and how it affects different areas of your body. Where is your gaze? Where is your mind?

From this standing position, mountain pose, raise your arms, bend your legs, and return to your forward fold. Repeat five times. Then connect all the poses together to create a moon salutation. Move through moon salutation a few times.

Here you have moon salutation. Now that it is yours, you can call on it any time you need support, whether emotional or physical. As you work through these poses, take your time to notice any messages your body has for you. Change the poses as your body asks for something different. Or do more of one pose and less of another. Add your old favorites. Make these poses your own. Find your own freedom and love in meditative movement.

Interlude

Breathing to Connect

This story is about how breath and mindfulness may be all we need.

Jacob was fifteen years old when he first walked into my classroom—a bubbly, chatty, outgoing, delightful teenager. I soon realized that beneath that happy facade coiled stirrings of distress. He had difficulty focusing, saw himself as stupid, and could hardly sit still long enough to finish a sentence. His parents faced challenges of their own. My meetings with his mother revealed her destructive self-hatred and desperate need for approval. His father was emotionally unavailable. I could see these qualities very clearly in them, because I carried them myself.

One sunny Los Angeles day, as I walked past the computer lab, a yellow shoelace caught my eye. I knew that shoelace, but it seemed to have been disconnected from its owner. It was sticking out from under a partition, and it was hard to imagine how Jacob or his shoe could be nearby. I paused for a moment, wondering if I should just let the shoelace rest. But something had to be wrong. I opened the glass door, closed it gently behind me, and then walked very audibly toward my destination. The shoelace did not move.

Jacob was sandwiched between two desks with privacy dividers running down to the floor. His position defied all laws of physics. I said nothing. Instead, I slid under a desk and lay there, inches from my student, with a partition between us. I could hear his sobs—muffled but deep. So I turned up the volume on my breathing: in, pause, out, pause. After a few minutes, his sobs abated and his breath started to join with mine; we stayed there for I don't know how many minutes.

Things seemed to have settled down when I heard some voices in the hallway. Without thinking, I held my breath. The door opened, and a group of families on a tour came in. In the next few seconds, I realized that Jacob had stopped breathing too. We both prayed for the gift of invisibility. After all, how would we explain our peculiar position? But our prayers paid off. After a minute, the group left and I heard the door close. We were never seen. To this day, I can't believe it. Maybe it's true that people only see what they want to see.

That interruption broke our meditation. We crawled out of our peaceful space and hugged. I wrote a note to Jacob's teacher. "Sorry, I delayed Jacob in the computer lab." A lie. The honest note, the one that his teacher would have puzzled over, would have said, "Jacob has been dealing with some difficulties and felt overwhelmed just now. He needed some time to cry, and so did I."

In a quite unexpected place, Jacob and I connected. No words were necessary. My experience with Jacob showed me the way breath and mindfulness, not words, can permit people to come together in new ways.

Meditation: Loving-Kindness

＊ ＊

This meditation invokes feelings of loving-kindness toward others and toward oneself. Some have likened the feelings aroused by this meditation to those of a mother as she cradles her drowsy infant. The image could just as well be of a father.

You will begin by offering loving-kindness to someone who has cared for you. We offer loving-kindness to others first because sometimes it is a challenge to offer love to ourselves. We doubt our worthiness and can manage to love ourselves only for a moment here and there. Yet without loving ourselves, we find it almost impossible to love others. So it is with others we must start. And in time, we find that loving others opens the door to our heart. There is no one more worthy of our love than ourselves.

The repetitive lines of this meditation may feel awkward at first. To me they did. At first, I found them forced and unnatural, and even a little silly. Yet over time, I was able to see that my initial reaction was just that: a *reaction*. When I started to question why I had such strong feelings about these words, the deeper meaning began to soak in, as water soaks into sand. When I felt the true meaning of the words for the first time, I wept. It's become a favorite meditation of mine. Just give it some time.

Find yourself a comfortable meditation position, and then begin to bring attention to your breath. Inhale and exhale as if you were using your heart for breathing rather than your lungs; breathe into your heart. (Consciously, breathe into your heart every day, and there you will find truth.) When you find yourself relaxed, begin the meditation.

As your eyes trace these phrases, speak them with an internal voice. Feel them resonate within. Repeat them as many times as you wish.

> May you, caregiver, be filled with loving-kindness.
> May you be well in body and mind.
> May you be safe from inner and outer harm.
> May you be truly happy and free.

Now shift the focus of your loving-kindness to yourself. Hold a picture of yourself as a vulnerable child in your heart, and allow the loving-kindness you want to bestow upon this child (you) to bubble up. Inwardly, recite the next phrases.

> May I be filled with loving-kindness.
> May I be well in body and mind.
> May I be safe from inner and outer harm.
> May I be truly happy and free.

Now, expand the focus of your heart to someone else that you love.

> May you, loved one, be filled with loving-kindness.
> May you be well in body and mind.
> May you be safe from inner and outer harm.
> May you be truly happy and free.

As you continue, you can gradually include others. Picture a friend, and bring these phrases of loving-kindness to him or her.

> May you, dear friend, be filled with loving-kindness.
> May you be well in body and mind.
> May you be safe from inner and outer harm.
> May you be truly happy and free.

Now, imagine all the people you know and care about, and bring loving-kindness to all, reciting as follows:

> May you all be filled with loving-kindness.
> May you all be well in body and mind.
> May you all be safe from inner and outer harm.
> May you all be truly happy and free.

Over time, you may feel ready to offer loving-kindness to those who hurt you. At first, you may feel only the pain that your memory holds. Approach this pain, inviting yourself to feel it without rancor. In time, you will see that keeping your heart closed to such people only causes you more suffering. You cannot live fully with parts of your heart closed.

When you are ready, visualize someone who has made your life more difficult, and then say the following words:

> May you, too, be filled with loving-kindness.
> May you, too, be well in body and mind.
> May you, too, be safe from inner and outer harm.
> May you, too, be truly happy and free.

Let the feelings of loving-kindness extend throughout the universe to all beings, young and old, human and animal, seen and unseen. Send loving-kindness to all of them.

> May every living thing be filled with loving-kindness.
> May every living thing be well in body and mind.
> May every living thing be safe from inner and outer harm.
> May every living thing be truly happy and free.

When you are ready, open your eyes and look upon the world with loving-kindness.

Journal Activity: Compassion for All

Write down five qualities of someone you dislike.

_____

_____

_____

How did you come to dislike these particular qualities?

_____

_____

_____

Write down five qualities of someone you like very much.

_____

_____

_____

How did you come to find these particular qualities likable?

_____

_____

_____

Take some deep breaths and find all of your honesty. Now answer the following question:

Can you see that the qualities listed above, both the likable and the disliked, are also qualities you posses? Touch any realizations with tender care. Write or draw below. Be curious about your reactions. Extend yourself love.

Closure

Our retreat has ended on a note of self-discovery. I know from all of the time I have spent with students and parents that the moment when a child leaves home resembles no other moment in the lifespan of a family. There is exaltation and sadness—and there is an opportunity to face oneself and one's loved ones and make a difference. You now have the tools to better understand your connection to your family. I've explained some of the impediments to a mindful, loving relation, and I've offered you pathways around judging and shaming. As you change your relation to yourself, you'll change that between you and those close to you—and to the world. It is not easy, and five days is only a beginning. But you will find in mindfulness a remarkable opening to parts of you that you thought were long completed. We are a work in progress, all of us. All we need is love.

An Ending?

As I walked along the forest path that connects my home to my favorite running trail, I saw the most extraordinary thing—tiny, delicate, safety-vest-orange mushrooms. I didn't know such a color existed in nature. What a wonder! I dropped to my knees to get a closer look, only to see more tiny heads pushing up out of the soil. What a gift!

It was a beautiful, hot, summer day. After staring for a time at my gift, I got back up and continued my run through the dappled shade a bit longer than usual. On my return, I looked for those little orange friends of mine but couldn't find them. Perhaps an animal had eaten them, or perhaps I had misremembered their exact home. I retraced my steps and poked around a bit until I found one, separate from the pack. Then I found the rest of the group, uprooted and kicked aside. What a shame! How could that be? Who would do such a thing?

Then it hit me. The mushrooms I saw on my path touched me differently than they did the person who had kicked them aside. My path—the things I find beautiful, and the things I care about—are unique to me. If I had run past those mushrooms on a rainy day, or when I was in a bad mood, my reaction might have been very different.

This book is my path, a path I have shared with parents and students over the years. Different activities speak more to some people than to others. And certain activities might make less sense now than they will in the future. In the end, your path to truth—to a better understanding of who you are—may diverge radically from the path laid out in this book. I'll be content if just one part of the book endures. I got an e-mail a while ago from a former student. Attached was a photo of him holding the hot-water bottle all students had received in my class. He was going through a tough time in graduate school and found comfort in its warmth and the memories it held. How simple and yet how terrific!

So where do you go from here? Go where your heart leads you. Just listen and look for signs. If you found that the movement exercises were meaningful to you, you might find a local yoga class or continue to do these simple moves yourself. If you resonated with the meditations, you might sit in meditation for a few minutes every day. If you choose to take a class, don't settle for one that doesn't speak to your truth or to the way you feel right now. As you grow to love yourself more deeply, the types of activities that will foster your self-growth will change. Just listen to your heart.

I encourage you to speak your truth. Honest communication is our opportunity to shine a light of awareness on those feelings we keep hidden from those we love and sometimes from ourselves. If someone's actions or words cause you discomfort, share your truth. The truth can sometimes make people uncomfortable, but truth pierces our hearts and opens us up to heal ourselves and our relationships. Share your truth with me at www.mindfulguidetocollegeprep.com.

Over the past year, I had to point out to one of my kids that one was manipulating the other. I had to admit that they learned that behavior from me, their mother. Opening and embracing my lack of awareness about myself is painful, but it leads to healing, which allows love to flow. These realizations invite me to a deeper understanding of humanity. I cannot think of anything better. Look for your truth in each moment of the day.

I've provided suggestions for further reading at the end of the book. These are things that have helped me in my own search and put me in touch with communities of mindful people who have supported my own path to self-growth. These may or may not be useful to you. Good luck, and please let me know how it goes.

Pull-Out Yoga Pose Sheet to Hang on Wall

1. Child's Pose   Extended Child's Pose   All Fours

2. All Fours   Face Down   All Fours

3. All Fours   Down Dog With Legs Bent   All Fours

4. Down Dog With Legs Bent   Forward Fold   Finger Tips

5. Finger Tips   Chair Pose   Mountain Pose

Suggested Reading

Boccio, Frank Jude. *Mindfulness Yoga: The Awakened Union of Breath, Body, and Mind*. Boston: Wisdom, 2004. This book showed me how to be in my body during yoga.

Brown, Brené. *The Gifts of Imperfection: Let Go of Who You Think You're Supposed to Be and Embrace Who You Are*. Center City, MN: Hazelden, 2010. The discussion of shame in this book opened my heart.

Brown, Stuart, with Christopher Vaughan. *Play: How It Shapes the Brain, Opens the Imagination, and Invigorates the Soul*. New York: Penguin, 2009. Research on play shows what we already know: play is a vital part of life.

Carr, Nicholas. *The Shallows: What the Internet Is Doing to Our Brains*. New York: W. W. Norton, 2010. This book brought up great questions about how we view our minds.

Goleman, Daniel. *Destructive Emotions: How Can We Overcome Them? A Scientific Dialogue with the Dalai Lama*. New York: Bantam Books, 2003. Goleman, through His Holiness the Dalai Lama, shines a light on what is truly important for humanity.

Greenland, Susan Kaiser. *The Mindful Child: How to Help Your Kid Manage Stress and Become Happier, Kinder, and More Compassionate*. New York: Free Press, 2010. Children are great educators, if we choose to listen.

Gunaratana, Bhante Henepola. *Mindfulness in Plain English*. Boston: Wisdom Publications, 2002. If you read only one book on meditation, let it be this one.

Hay, Louise L. *Heal Your Body: The Mental Causes for Physical Illness and the Metaphysical Way to Overcome Them*. Santa Monica, CA: Hay House, 1988. This book helps open us to the relationship between our minds and our health.

Hendrix, Harville. *Getting the Love You Want: A Guide for Couples.* New York: Holt, 2008. This dialogue technique succeeds because our families and loved ones are our healers.

Iyengar, B. K. S. *Light on Yoga.* New York: Schocken, 1977. A clear guide to yoga.

Kabat-Zinn, Jon. *Full Catastrophe Living: Using the Wisdom of Your Body and Mind to Face Stress, Pain, and Illness.* New York: Delacorte, 1990. Our bodies' wisdom is at center stage, gently inviting us to listen.

Miller, Alice. *For Your Own Good: Hidden Cruelty in Child-Rearing and the Roots of Violence.* New York: Farrar, Straus, Giroux, 1983. An eye-opening look at how we raise our children.

Rumi, Jalal al-Din. *The Love Poems of Rumi.* Edited by Deepak Chopra. New York: Harmony, 1998. Simply beautiful.

Salzberg, Sharon. *Loving-Kindness: The Revolutionary Art of Happiness.* Boston: Shambhala, 2002. Prepare to be embraced by pure love and light.

Smalley, Susan L., and Diana Winston. *Fully Present: The Science, Art, and Practice of Mindfulness.* Cambridge, MA: Da Capo Lifelong, 2010. Here is the support you need to meditate for a lifetime.

Sood, Amit. *Train Your Brain, Engage Your Heart, Transform Your Life: A Two Step Program to Enhance Attention; Decrease Stress; Cultivate Peace, Joy and Resilience; and Practice Presence with Love.* Rochester, MN: Morning Dew, 2010. Forgiveness, gratitude, and love can heal our bodies and release us from pain.

Printed in the United States
By Bookmasters